Letters to Jack Tait

T0099795

Letters to Jack Tait

A Psychologist Looks Back

Pat Tait

authorHOUSE®

AuthorHouse™
1663 Liberty Drive
Bloomington, IN 47403
www.authorhouse.com
Phone: 1-800-839-8640

© 2011 Pat Tait. All rights reserved.

No part of this book may be reproduced, stored in a retrieval system, or transmitted by any means without the written permission of the author.

First published by AuthorHouse   08/20/2011

ISBN: 978-1-4567-9608-2 (sc)

Printed in the United States of America

Any people depicted in stock imagery provided by Thinkstock are models, and such images are being used for illustrative purposes only.
Certain stock imagery © Thinkstock.

This book is printed on acid-free paper.

Because of the dynamic nature of the Internet, any web addresses or links contained in this book may have changed since publication and may no longer be valid. The views expressed in this work are solely those of the author and do not necessarily reflect the views of the publisher, and the publisher hereby disclaims any responsibility for them.

INTRODUCTION

Dear Jack Tait,

Allow me to introduce you to these letters from your great-grandfather Dr. Pat Tait, and to myself. My name is Tony Chesterman and I have been acting as Pat's editor during the writing of these letters. He and I have known each other for a long time.

We first met in 1964. I was the new curate in the parish where Pat was a GP partner in a local medical practice. In addition to being newly ordained I was also newly married to my wife Valerie. These were new roles for us, to which we subsequently added the role of parent. Unsurprisingly we encountered problems from time to time and the persons we mostly turned to for help were Pat and Dorothy Tait.

They obliged us to face up to the implications of our own psychological make-up, and to the issues arising from the new roles we were exercising. Their combined insights and wisdom, especially in relation to the vital importance of loving parenting, we recall with gratitude to this day. You too will discover that the importance of parental love, especially that of a mother, runs like a golden thread through these letters.

Why did Pat write them? Principally because he wanted to take an honest (at times brutally honest) look at his life and work in order to pass on to you, and others who might read these letters, what really matters if human beings are to be truly human.

I commend them to you and wish you every blessing.

Yours sincerely,

Canon Tony Chesterman.

TOPICS

HELLO

Dear Jack Tait,

I write this on January the sixth 2009. You are three years old and I am 90. I am the last of the family to bear the Tait name, and were it not for the thoughtful and much appreciated action of your parents in giving you the name, it would disappear.

I'm not going to write an autobiography because that would be extremely boring for me to write and for you to read, but I would like to share with you significant aspects of my life, and the insights I have gained. If you do find it boring just turn the page! I suppose I'm writing to give you some idea of the sort of person I was.

I am the youngest of three. My brother was seven years older than me, and my sister ten. As I was born in 1918 I often wondered if I was my parents' response to the wastage of life in World War 1, but I actually do not think my conception was planned! I was born, educated, and medically trained in Edinburgh. After qualification, at the age of 23, I spent nine months in hospital as a junior doctor, then 4 years in the Navy as a Surgeon Lieutenant. It was during that time that my interest in psychological medicine developed to the extent that I was all set to become a psychiatrist. After demobilisation in 1946 I took a job in a mental hospital, and it cured me! I found that I did not want to work with mentally ill people but with ordinary folk who were unhappy, so I became a GP where I would meet people at first hand and not after they had been filtered through a psychiatric net.

As a GP in North Derbyshire I found that the insights of the great psychological researchers, Jung, Freud and Adler did not necessarily seem to apply to the people who came into my surgery. So I realized that I would have to start from scratch and work out why those unhappy people who came to see me, were in fact unhappy. During my time as a GP I came to understand why people were depressed, angry, frightened and feeling useless, and something of what I discovered will appear in later pages.

My psychological thinking was much influenced by some great modern psychologists. My first "great" is Harry Harlow.

Yours fondly,

Pat

Dorothy

just after we were married, 1953

My Mother

HARLOW

Dear Jack,

Harry Harlow was the first contemporary psychologist I had any knowledge of and I came across him by accident, reading an article in the weekly news magazine 'Picture Post', long since defunct. But it was our experience with Ben, (about whom I write later), that made me realise how important his work was and why I include him in my pantheon of "greats."

I did not know much about the man until I read a biography of him intriguingly called 'Love at Goon Park' by Professor Debra Blum, an account of the development of psychological thinking from the 1950s onwards. She makes it clear that Harry Harlow, in his experiments using monkeys, was in effect exploring the quality of mother love and confirming its vital importance.

In the 1950s Harlow became Professor of Psychology at Wisconsin University at a time when a lot of research into human behaviour was done by people who thought that running rats in mazes would reveal the secrets of the human mind (apart from John Bowlby and a few others.) These psychological explorers considered babies not to have emotions, rather they were merely motivated by hunger and nipple seeking reflexes. Harlow did not agree and after watching the behaviour of monkeys at a local zoo he realized they had a range of emotions similar to ours, and that it would be much more informative to work with them rather than rats. (He called the psychologists working with rats "rodentologists"!) However, healthy monkeys were hard to come by so he started a breeding programme to produce a supply of healthy monkeys. This he did, very successfully, but it involved separating the baby monkeys from their mothers to keep them free from infection. He then had to cope with lots of very unhappy motherless babies. There then followed his famous experiment.

He put into a cage containing a baby monkey a wire frame holding a feeding bottle and another similar frame, but this one was covered with soft woolly material. He found that the baby monkey would often cling to the woolly frame when it was hungry rather than feed from the bare wire frame, thereby dramatically demonstrating the importance of the touching of mother loving. I was particularly interested in the effects of this maternal deprivation on the personality of the monkeys when they grew up. The adult females were unfriendly, hostile, antisocial, showed no affection for their offspring and had actually been known to murder them. They could only be mated, to quote Harlow, by a persistent and athletic male. This finding immediately made me wonder to what extent the antisocial behaviour of today's young is a result of a lack of mother loving. Harlow was much criticized by animal rights people because of the way he treated his baby monkeys and as a result little attention was paid to his work. I'm glad to say that his researches are now receiving the attention they deserve.

My story starts when, as an assistant GP, I was asked to make an urgent visit to an outlying smallholding, where a domestic drama was taking place. When I got there I found the daughter of the house (who I will call Mary D), standing in a corner of the kitchen holding a large carving knife apparently having been threatening to kill her mother, who was standing in the opposite corner. I had walked in on a potentially dangerous situation and to calm things down I asked the mother to leave us, leaving me alone with a very angry young woman. She was a buxom, sunburned 17 year-old who calmed down once her mother had left. The only thing I could think of doing was to get her to come and see me in the surgery the next day, where we could talk on neutral ground. I then sought out her parents waiting in the front room. Two tall, thin, grey people quietly standing and waiting. I told them what I had arranged and they seemed relieved. They asked no questions and showed no emotion. So, having told them that I was going to work with their daughter, I departed.

The story the girl told me later was that she was an only child who spent most of her time helping her father run the smallholding. She had no memory of ever having had any kisses or cuddles from either parent. She told me she had outbursts of uncontrollable anger and hostility directed at her mother. That she had never had a boyfriend and had no interest in men. After several sessions, when I thought we had talked through her problems sufficiently and I had taught her how to control her anger, she decided she felt better and so the 'treatment' was over and she departed. That was the last I saw of her. I did not realize at the time that she was the human counterpart of a grown up un-mothered monkey! The fact is that if a mother does not treat her baby with the cuddles, strokes and chuckles that are part and parcel of mother loving, as far as a baby is concerned, it is motherless.

Several years later my wife Dorothy, a trained and experienced nursery nurse, was asked by the social worker attached to the local maternity unit, if she would foster a 10 day old baby boy called Ben who had been completely rejected by his mother. Apparently she would not hold him, touch him, cuddle him or even bottle feed him. The story went that she had hated being pregnant and had had a very stormy pregnancy during which she suffered from persistent vomiting. Once her child was born she would have nothing to do with it. So the unfortunate child was looked after by the midwives on duty, who could only see that he was properly fed.

Dorothy agreed to the fostering and so the day came when the social worker brought the waif to us and laid him on our bed. We were both shocked by what we saw. He lay motionless, making no sound, with a pale face and a strange half smile on his face. I had never seen a 10 day old baby look so ill. Dorothy's immediate reaction was to pick him up and cuddle him. She continued to cuddle him for the next three months. At night he slept by her side in a rocking cot, so that she could rock him back to sleep if she heard him wake.

From that time the two of them were inseparable. She did her house work with him on her hip. He particularly enjoyed being bathed. So into the bath he went, sometimes three times a day. Gradually our foster child was transformed into a noisy, pink cheeked, smiling character who wriggled with pleasure when he saw Dorothy. It was a very sad day for us when the adopting parents came to collect him. (His mother continued to refuse to have anything to do with him and so adoption had been arranged.) It took us both some time to get over the departure of a small person we had come to love.

It was only after his arrival that I discovered that Mary D was his mother! When I had worked with her I had not remembered Harry Harlow, but as soon as I realized who she was, a light dawned and I realised that I had been involved with the human equivalent of one of Harry Harlow's motherless female adult monkeys. I particularly remembered a photograph of such a monkey holding her child at arms length with her face turned away from it. Mary D had really needed re-parenting, not just a few chats with a friendly doctor. I heard later that she had become an alcoholic and died of liver failure. Altogether a very sad story.

Harry Harlow was a rebel fighting for the rights of women and the importance of their loving. As far as English society is concerned it looks as if it is badly in need of a reminder of the importance of mother loving. Harry Harlow's motherless male babies turned into psychopathic adults equally capable of damaging or murdering their own children.

This was my first experience of an affectionless family and what happened to a child born into it. It was astonishing how much damage could be done to a baby during the first 10 days of its life, damage that it took three months of tender loving care to put right. Having thought that human psychology started in the early years of childhood, I now knew that it started at the very beginning.

Yours fondly,

Pat

Me,
posing for a newspaper photograph
circa 1960

Honor; my first wife

3

MIND AND BODY

Dear Jack,

When I started in general practice I was convinced that the concept of mind and body as separate entities was mistaken. As far as I was concerned, the emotions influenced the body and had a hand in the development of organic disease, and the bodily states influenced our emotions. It seems I was an early example of a doctor interested in holistic medicine.

After the war, psychosomatic medicine was deemed to be a load of rubbish, not being based on a series of double blind trials but rather on the personal experience of people working directly with patients. In spite of that view it seemed to make a lot of sense to me, and in the surgery, having had a lot of experience of organic diseases, I remained convinced that emotions played a considerable part in their development. One theory maintained that repressed anger played a part in the development of arthritis so I set about exploring this. One of my patients was a bus driver who had a melodious voice, which I came to associate with arthritics, and who had had to give up his job because of increasing pain and stiffness in his fingers. I talked to him about his anger and he told me he never ever got angry. When I suggested that he might try and let off steam by shouting or hitting a pillow, his response was to say, "What have I got to be angry about? I couldn't do that." He ended up in a wheelchair, his voice as melodious as ever. My experience with him was repeated many times and the only way I could understand the connection was to suppose that the energy of anger was locked up in those parts of the body used to express it, namely bones and muscles, which are not designed by evolution to store up such energy and which consequently broke down.

On another occasion I was giving a lecture to a group of about 30 pre-retirement people about the problems anger could cause when two people, for the first time in their lives, spend all their time together. I asked for a show of hands of those who suffered from muscular aches and pains or arthritis and some hands went up. I then asked for a show of hands for those people who never got angry and to the surprise of all of us the same hands went up, including that of a man who I realized was sitting in a wheelchair. The convener of the meeting told me later that he suffered from rheumatoid arthritis and that after my lecture he had got out of his wheelchair and gone back to work! I couldn't help wondering whether he had had a sudden explosion of anger, releasing the energy locked up in his bones and muscles, but I shall never know, so I could only give myself a half-hearted 'Pat' on the back.

Another interesting idea was that suppressed grief played a part in the development of asthma. I confirmed that people with asthma did not cry easily but I failed to do what had been claimed, namely, curing an attack of asthma by making people cry. However I did confirm that people who could cry easily did not suffer from asthma.

Civilisation has determined that anger and aggression are anti-social and must be kept in check, but in recent years this check, namely a fear of authority and reprisals, has markedly diminished with a consequent increase in antisocial behaviour. From strict Victorian patriarchal control we have moved into an anti-authoritarian mood in society and a ridiculous upholding of 'human rights' which means that everyone has the right to behave badly, a very unhappy state of affairs.

Repressed anger causes physical illness. Anger expressed causes rows, physical conflict and murder. There are socially acceptable ways of releasing anger like shouting and behaving badly at football matches. But anger is never caused by someone else, it is triggered by them. The anger is our own and we should take responsibility for it and find ways of releasing its energy without causing harm, hence the value of football matches! I wish I knew whether, as a consequence, the incidence of arthritis had diminished!

An intriguing insight emerged that if anger is repressed at the stage when it is just a concept and before the biochemical process actually begins, the result is a migraine headache. If it is repressed as soon as the physiological changes start, the result is persistent high blood pressure, and if it is repressed when muscles are about to explode, the consequence is arthritis. I found this a very interesting theory and in practice would try to find out if people with recurrent headaches had any buried anger. These were occasions when my digging proved helpful although the result was that apparently peaceful people became angry. But free from headaches! I was developing methods of psychological archaeology! I would do the same digging with hypertensives and arthritics but often never felt that my efforts were particularly valuable.

In the case of repressed grief (as in those social situations in which expressions of emotion are discouraged), the consequences, particularly in childhood, can be chronic coughs and colds and possibly asthma. I also noticed that the children of very house-proud mothers often had eczema, which some said was another result of repressed anger.

'Proper' doctors will have nothing to do with such theories and that included my GP colleagues. They would much rather search for physical causes and find drugs to counteract them.

But I want to tell you a story about a lady I know very well. One day she went to visit her mother, taking her two daughters with her. Shortly after their arrival, her mother launched into a tirade, accusing her of not bringing her children up properly, of not dressing them properly, and she went on and on. My friend, being a dutiful daughter, endured the onslaught silently, offering no defence (after all, you are taught to love your Mother so it wouldn't be right to argue with her!) She collected her daughters and left. When she got home she found she had an excruciating attack of what was then called 'fibrositis' in her right shoulder. She came to see us the same evening and told us about her painful shoulder. I asked her what had been going on that day and she told us about the horrible visit to her mother and all the criticism. I asked for a little more detail and what she was feeling about it all. She was about to tell us when she suddenly burst out: "I am bloody angry! Bugger my mother, bugger the old bitch!", and more in the same vein. When she had calmed down, she said: "That's funny, the pain's gone!" A validation of a theory, and before my very eyes!

Books have played a central part in determining the direction in which I wanted to go, so when I came across one called 'Getting Well Again', which was about defeating cancer using a variety of psychological techniques, such as meditation, relaxation and guided imagery, I thought it was time to stop theorising about cancer, and do something practical. So, with the help of a lady teacher, who had had both breasts removed and was in remission, and with my wife, I started a cancer support group. Most of the people who came had already been through the therapeutic mill (chemotherapy, radiotherapy, surgery) and were either in remission or involved in a second round of treatment. I was, of course, most interested in the emotional state of the people who came and it became obvious that nearly all suffered from the deadly disease of 'niceness', which means, among other things, that the sufferer cannot say "No!" without feeling guilty. (There is an excellent book called just that.) The mask they wore was so thick that any efforts of their negative emotions to penetrate it were of no avail, and I discovered that this was often the case with people who had cancer. Introducing the group to their Mr Hydes was a hilarious experience. Such surprise and pleasure on discovering that they could vent their anger without upsetting anybody and, what was more, stand up for themselves and find the courage to ask their consultants all the questions they had been too afraid to ask before. It also meant the end of their approval hunger and the end of being 'nice' people! In order to achieve the peace of mind that I felt was so important if the immune system was to work properly in its attack on cancer cells, I got the group to do a mental spring clean, to finish any unfinished business in their lives, to repair fractured relationships (especially with partners and relatives) and to seek out and make contact with old friends

I was influenced by Zen Buddhism to think that we should be able to bring all of ourselves into the now, the present moment. In order to be able to do this we must try to be free from worries from the past reaching into our present, and our present being disturbed by anxieties about the future. These have been called afterburn and reachback and it is obvious that there can be no peace of mind until these are dealt with.

And then there was death, and it quickly transpired that it was not actually death that bothered people, but the manner of dying, especially if helpless and in pain. I had done some work in the local hospice so I could be reassuring about the way the hospice movement had revolutionized medical attitudes about pain relief and the care that was taken to see that people could end their lives peacefully and pain free. Discussing death led to discussions of belief systems, often the first time that people had had an opportunity to talk about what they believed in. Especially angels!

I don't think this group work cured anybody but it did seem to help them face their futures more comfortably and to die more easily. After 14 years the group ended. The numbers had dwindled and there were no new recruits. We were glad. Putting it bluntly, we had had enough of death.

The lady, with whom I started the group, was a teacher of infants whom she loved dearly and who loved her. When her contract ended the powers that be refused to renew it because of her medical history. She died within three months. It seemed to me that her love for the children and their love for her, had kept her alive.

Yours fondly,

Pat

My Parents and I - mid-teens

Dorothy in the Morris Minor

Dorothy and I
with our first caravan: a Barclay Caravette

4

BERNE

Dear Jack,

The skeleton in my cupboard is the fact that my father died in a mental hospital in Edinburgh. He was suffering from what in those days was called manic depressive psychosis, now bi-polar illness. What worried me about this was the fact that it could be inherited and therefore it was probable that I had inherited the gene. But I discovered you could only inherit the tendency to have the illness, not the illness itself. For this to develop there had to be an emotional trigger, a toxic programme in the mind with sufficient energy to waken the gene and then cause the illness. That being so, I was determined to do everything in my power to let the gene remain asleep. I was spurred on by the fact that I had had periods of depression already. It was the psychologist Eric Berne who made it possible for me to search out such a malign programme and to overcome a very powerful personal daemon.

I think he was one of the 20th century's foremost psychologists, (once I had freed myself from the idea that Freud, Jung and Adler had written all there was to know about psychology). Finding that the people who came into my surgery had psychologies that were quite different from what these great men had described, I had to start from scratch and find out for myself what was going on inside my patients. Berne, without any psychobabble, introduced me to some ideas that I immediately thought hit the mark and went straight into my head and immediately became part of my psychological furniture. I thought that I had joined a band of pioneers! Of course, after Berne there were many others but he was the 'Great Liberator'.

The great thing he did for me was to provide a simple, logical description of the way the mind worked. He said that in every mind there existed a series of what he called 'ego states'. Different states of mind to which he gave the names, Parent, Adult and Child.

There are two aspects to the Parent ego state—Critical and Nurturing. The Critical Parent is an inner voice that either criticizes others, or oneself, in a finger-pointing way. I could identify with this immediately because I had suffered tremendously from my own self-criticism which told me that I was no good and an unlikeable failure; the voice that precipitated my attacks of depression! He said that this voice was an accumulation of all the critical things that had been said about us and that we had said about ourselves when we were children, all bundled together. Thankfully this voice was not genetically determined but merely a record of things said, and as such it could be erased and with Berne's help, I managed to do this. He taught me to recognize the voice of my Critical Parent and then tell him to get the hell out of my head. Which made me feel that I had got out of prison! (And incidentally I found I had left my inferiority complex behind and for the first time could regard myself as a perfectly normal member of the human race). The Nurturing Parent is genetically determined and plays a vital role in the creation of loving families. Its function is to protect the very young and act as a role model for the growing child, teaching it how to cope with the outside world.

Then there is the Adult, the unemotional voice of common sense, the problem-solver, the communicator, the scientist, the mathematician. The Critical Parent speaks with a hectoring bullying voice, the Adult is cool, calm and collected. I found that some people would often insist that they were in their Adult ego state whilst using a loud voice, which always gave the game away.

The final member of our internal dramatis personae is the Inner Child which, like the Parent, has two different aspects. The first is what Berne called the Adapted Child, meaning that as children we have to adapt to survive in the family we were born into and that this child is still alive in us, often miserable, angry, frightened and whiney. When I am being petulant or irritable it always means I have been taken over by my Adapted Child.

The other part of the Inner Child Berne called the Free Child, the fun loving affectionate and spontaneous part of us that is our birthright but which is so often crushed and can remain locked up inside us. In which case we have a 'shut-out child' and a life with no fun and, worst of all, a dislike of Star Trek! And in my experience a considerable risk of developing organic disease.

Berne called this model of the mind Structural Analysis and his way of working was to study people's behaviour towards each other in groups. The interaction between two people he called a 'transaction'. Pleasant chatter between two people he called 'pastimes'. But repeating patterns that were really contests between a winner and a loser, he called 'games'. He wrote a compendium describing these games which he called 'Games People Play', and to his great surprise it was a bestseller. I found some of the games he described so funny (in an 'unfunny' way) and so frequently encountered that I think it is worth describing one or two. 'Why don't you . . . . Yes but!' is a game played by two people one of whom wants to be helpful and the other doesn't want to be helped, but pretends that he/she does. The helpful person, who Berne calls the Rescuer, gives some advice "Why don't you leave him, divorce him, get a lover etc," and the other says in effect "Oh, I can't do that because . . . .", which shows that the rescuer is batting on a sticky wicket because the person he/she is trying to help is perfectly happy in the state they are in and can happily play another game called 'Ain't it Awful'. Which is about trying to 'hook' another rescuer who will be sorry for them. (This game is always played with an easily recognisable whiny voice.) Then there is 'Now I've Got You, You Son Of A Bitch.' For the sake of convenience this one is shortened to 'Nigysob' and is a favourite game played by bullies. He/she waits until there is a flaw in the argument of the other and then fastens on it with cries of joy. The people who play 'Ain't it Awful' are usually female Victims married to Persecutors who spend a lot of their time in their Critical Parent, behaving badly while they try to destroy her self-confidence and self-respect.

The three types of people I have described, Persecutors, Rescuers and Victims have each found a role that satisfies their emotional needs and which they do not wish to give up. They are adept at involving people in the games they want to play and will try to 'hook' someone into playing the game so that they will get yet another dose of the emotional food they desire so much. The Victim gets another dose of sympathy, the Persecutor another dose of dominance and the Rescuer an ego boosting dose of gratitude. There is no fun in any of these damaging games and it was my lot as a psychotherapist for people to try and hook me into playing the Rescuer, and by people playing 'Aint it Awful'. I became skilful at escaping the hook.

Berne was a blast of fresh air. Out went the old psychologies and in came the new. However, I did not throw the baby out with the bathwater because much of what Jung, in particular, said has stayed with me.

The great thing about Berne was that both his Structural Analysis and his Transactional Analysis could be talked about with a complete absence of psychobabble, which I hated.

Yours fondly,

Pat

Me, aged about 3 years

David
on receiving
a Good Conduct Medal

5

AWARENESS

Dear Jack,

In my early days as a GP I owned a soft-top Morris Minor. It was one of the early ones with a side valve engine and not much performance, so I decided to see if I could make it go faster. I had a high compression aluminium cylinder head fitted and twin carburettors and its performance was vastly improved. But because it had an inadequate cooling system, (it had no water pump), it overheated and so I had to drive it very sensibly. My ambition had overcome my commonsense. If when I had lifted up the bonnet I had fully understood the workings of the engine I would not have been so silly. The moral of this story is that if we want to make ourselves work better, we must do the equivalent and become aware of what goes on inside our heads. (The Buddhist thinks that self-awareness, which he would call 'mindfulness', is one of the most important things to learn in the journey towards perfection).

Carl Gustav Jung took a great interest in the work of the alchemists, (who were really forerunners of modern-day scientists and psychologists), and the process they used in their search for the secret of turning base materials into gold, (taking the raw materials of the human mind and trying to perfect it?). They put all their ingredients in a crucible and then lit a fire under it. The alchemical process started when the contents went black, known as the process of the 'blackening'. Jung said that on the journey towards self actualization, which he called individuation, there had to be the 'blackening', a good name for the painful experience of seeing ourselves as we really are.

It had never occurred to me that I might sometimes behave badly because I assumed, without thinking, that my behaviour was acceptable. But when I began to think about the difference between good behaviour and bad behaviour, a subject I had never thought about before, I decided that good behaviour made people either happy or well and that bad behaviour made them either ill or miserable. As you will discover in these letters, I found the truth about my own behaviour very upsetting. The 'blackening' had started.

Jung said that the mind had four functions, thinking, feeling, sensing, and intuiting, which tells us what to look for when we lift up the bonnet. What do I think about? What do I feel? What do I sense? What is my intuition telling me? It is interesting that we can be aware of what we are thinking, and of sensations and feeling but not so easily aware of our intuitions which communicate with us very quietly. So it is as if we are sitting on our own shoulder and looking in, to see what's happening inside our heads. Our ability to do this must mean that although we have these four functions, we have them but we are not them. It is as if we are just a still centre into which information from these four functions is fed. The Buddhist emphasises the value of meditation, a technique which allows us to make contact with our still centre by concentrating on breathing. But I found that I was more interested in the reasons why I needed to meditate rather than the meditation itself.

One exercise in awareness involves going for a walk and at first becoming aware of everything that it is possible to see, upwards, downwards and from side to side. While doing this, become aware of everything that it is possible to hear, then become aware of everything you can feel, the wind in your face, the touch of clothing and your feet on the ground, and then what you can taste. The great Russian thinker Ouspensky, who described this exercise, suggested that we suck a peppermint and inwardly recite some poetry while doing all of the above. This I have never been able to do but I have enjoyed the exercise of the senses and the feeling of alertness that follows.

My peace of mind was easily disturbed by unwanted emotion which like my absent water pump made my own engine run hot. There were situations that made me frightened and anxious, encounters that make me angry, and memories that made me sad. The most obtrusive feelings were those of inadequacy and inferiority, and the anger that bubbled up inside me if I felt somebody was trying to dominate me, a reaction I could trace back to the way my bossy big sister treated me.

At about that time there was a great interest in the beneficial effects of physical relaxation and in helping people to control panic states. I thought I had better learn something about it. To my pleasure, I found that it worked. I discovered that the most helpful technique was one which helped people feeling the onset of a panic attack while shopping in a supermarket to relax, there and then. A relaxation routine which required people either to lie down or sit comfortably tended to induce a trance, which although very enjoyable was not much use when out shopping! I used to get people to imagine that they were a sack of potatoes with a hole in the bottom out of which potatoes were dribbling and the sack gradually collapsing from the top down. I happened to notice that if I was working with a patient in the surgery and began to get irritated, my right fist would clench and that if I relaxed it my irritability would vanish.

Buddha, having decided that the purpose of life was to journey towards perfection, proceeded to provide his disciples with a handbook. First he enunciated the 'Four Noble Truths'. I have put in brackets my psychological interpretation:

1. Life is suffering. (We live under the influence of our Deprivation Psychology.).
2. 2. Suffering is due to attachment. (Our psychology won't change unless we work at it.).
3. Attachment can be overcome. (We can work at it.).
4. There is a path for accomplishing this, which is one way of saying that there is hope for everybody.

He then proceeds to give instructions to those on the path about how to walk it. They had to aim for:

1. Right View (Have a good idea about where you're going.)
2. Right Intention (Keep your mind on the job.)

3. Right Speech (Words are powerful, for good or ill.)
4. Right Action (Behave ethically.)
5. Right Livelihood (Work at something fulfilling not self-destructive.).
6. Right Effort (Keep at it.)
7. Right Mindfulness (Work at your self awareness.)
8. Right Concentration (Don't muck about.)

Having read these instructions I came to the conclusion that the Buddha knew what he was talking about. He was a good psychologist and what he said 500 years before the birth of Christ has not lost its significance and freshness today. But like all the great religions, the central messages tend to be taken over by the organizers who make the ritual the thing and not the central message.

A tailpiece fantasy. An elderly white-haired bloke wearing pink trousers and a blue shirt was examining a rather ancient soft top Morris Minor. He saw that the bodywork had quite a few dents and scratches and that where there had been rust it had been not very expertly repaired, but adequately. The front seats were worn but in good order but the back was cluttered with books, some new, some old which tumbled off the back seat onto the floor. The boot was filled with a multitude of discarded electronic gadgets. Loudspeakers, tuners, amplifiers, old mobile phones and goodness knows what else. Walking round to the front, he lifted up the bonnet and saw with pleasure that a water pump had been fitted, so obviously it had been running cooler. The engine was far from spotless but was reasonably clean and pulling out the dipstick he saw that the oil in the sump, although not completely clean would last a few more miles before it needed changing. I did say that this was a fantasy!

Yours fondly,

Pat

Erica

HMS Sussex, on which I served druing WWII

6

MASLOW

Dear Jack,

This letter is about a psychologist who has made a great impression on me. As well as being a psychologist he was a philosopher and a metaphysician. He acted as a compass giving me a bearing for the direction in which I wanted to go, a framework which helped to me to organize my thoughts, which up to then had been filed in an untidy heap.

I think Abraham Maslow was the first and perhaps the only psychologist to study the psychology of happy people and as a result said there was not just one psychology but two, one of happiness and one of unhappiness. (My interpretation.). He called them Being Psychology and Deprivation Psychology. The first described the state of mind of people who had become fully developed, what he called Self-actualized. These people were friendly, generous, altruistic, empathetic and creative: characteristics which although latent in all of us only develop if all our emotional needs are met, in other words if we are loved enough when we are children. (Again my interpretation, not Maslow's.)

Deprivation Psychology develops in us when we are not loved enough. The human race has a long history of treating newly born babies very badly. Carl Gustav Jung thought that memories of this are still present in the human psyche in a deep area that he called the Collective Unconscious because it is a part of the mind that we all share. Not an easy concept to take on board but it can account for the nameless fear that underlies and precipitates the development of Deprivation Psychology. The majority of us are under the influence of Deprivation Psychology, simply because our parents were not perfect people. It is a sad fact that the newly born baby needs more loving than its parents are usually able to give it.

It is easy to criticize people under the influence of their Deprivation Psychology for being 'selfish'. They certainly have needed to be self-centred to survive, but the survival lessons learned in childhood unfortunately persist into adult life where they restrict our ability to keep on growing. To escape and be free from such negative programmes they have to be recognized, confronted and worked through before we can be free of them. I made up an allegory to illustrate this:

The alien fell to earth because his spaceship stopped functioning. He found that he was near a great jungle out of which came the growls and snarls of large animals which he thought would probably eat him up. So he erected a forcefield round in the area within which he thought he could live, but at night the animals came out of the jungle and tried to leap over the forcefield so he made it higher. He lived happily within his forcefield but one day he said to himself "I am getting to be an old alien and will probably soon die so I might as well find out what is outside my forcefield, even if it means being eaten up by wild animals". So he dismantled his forcefield and found to his surprise that the jungle was no longer there, nor were there any wild animals. He thought "if I had not been so frightened I would have done this a long time ago, what a silly alien I am!" In this way our childish fears can persist when in reality there is nothing to be afraid of.

I have long thought that life is a journey, part of which is to encounter and accept the bad within us while striving for perfection, rather like a knight of old setting out on his quest for the Grail or the Pearl of Great Price; in our case the True Self. The Pearl is hidden in the depths of a deep and dark cave (the unconscious), it's entrance being guarded by a Dragon which must be slain (representing the unloving mother!) A journey from hate to love. Thus Maslow has marked out the beginning and the end of the journey. We start with our Deprivation Psychology and journey towards the goal of becoming who we really are, into a state of Being.

Philip Larkin, in his notorious poem 'This Be The Verse' writes "They *muck you up, your mum and dad, They do not mean to, but they do, They fill you with the faults they had, And add some extra just for you." (* He used a rather ruder word!) This enables me to say that we start our journey "mucked up" and our goal is to become "un-mucked up". I used to recite this poem to my patients in order make it clear that we are all in the same boat, even a psychotherapist! Maslow described this journey as the process of self-actualisation. I will write about some of the characteristics of Deprivation Psychology later.

Walking in a local park the other day I was impressed by the beauty and symmetry of trees that stood alone compared to distorted and cramped shapes of trees that grew in an over populated wood. One was being itself, and the other, cramped and distorted by being deprived of adequate space. I wished I could be like that stand-alone tree.

Yours fondly,

Pat

Dorothy and Me

Timothy

7

FAMILY

Dear Jack,

It must be obvious to you that I am very happy talking about my experiences as a doctor but not so happy talking about my family, but I suppose the time has come when I must write about it.

Let me start with my father. As I have said before he was a bipolar alcoholic with no fondness for his children. There is one experience that haunts me to this day. I was standing outside the Students' Union with a group of friends when a rather raggedly dressed man approached me and asked me if I could give him some money to buy cigarettes. I gave him what was in my pocket and then turned away and rejoined my friends. That man was my father and the meeting evoked no emotional response in me. I had no further contact with him and some months later was informed that he had died and would I go and identify the body, which I duly did, and that was the end of my relationship with him. I did have some happy memories like the time when he asked me to help him make a catapult which he constructed very skilfully using chamois leather, waxed thread and square section elastic. He was a farmer's son who grew up in Warwickshire where he learned to fish, shoot and poach pheasants, hence the catapult. I do not remember any praise or encouragement from him.

Before his emotional instability took over his life and ruined his business, he had become a very respected what was then called a ' fire assessor ' and is now called a loss adjuster, specialising in farm fires. He spoke little of his past but I know he was a first-class athlete and had played hockey for his county. He was intensely competitive and was very jealous of my brother. For instance, when playing golf with him he tried to put him off his stroke by moving or whistling. However, the havoc wrought on family life by a bipolar alcoholic is best understood by considering my attitude towards him after the encounter outside the Union.

My relationship with my mother was always friendly but she too was not a loving woman and when at the end of her life she was badly disabled by a stroke, I was unmoved. I did not seem to be capable of feeling affection.

My first marriage was the outcome of a student friendship. I was a final year medical student and she was a bright intelligent lass doing an Arts degree. The friendship broke up when I joined the Navy and as a result of an experience that I had in Durban in 1944 when a very loving lady refused to accept that I was sexually incompetent and proceeded to demonstrate that I was wrong! Before this encounter I had been quite sure that marriage for me was out of the question. It now became a possibility and I knew who I would like to marry. This was the girl I mentioned above. I proposed to her via an air mail letter and was accepted by return. We married soon after my return to the UK. The marriage did not turn out very well because I expected her to have the housewifely abilities possessed by my mother and of which she had none. I became irritable, critical and abusive. I'm sure my behaviour did much to destroy her self-esteem. Her happiest times were when she was pregnant with our three children but once they were born she had little idea of how to care for them, and I likewise demonstrated a complete lack of parental care. She died during the poliomyelitis epidemic of 1952 and I am certain that my treatment of her played a part in her death. As I have said in another letter, it was only after she had died that I fully understood how badly I had treated her. I decided then and there that although I could not change the past I could spend my future trying to make amends by helping people to be happy. After her death Dorothy came to help me look after the children and ultimately became my much loved second wife.

Of my two sons the younger, Timothy, was my favourite and, as fathers do, I thought he was the one who would follow in my footsteps and become a doctor. But lacking as I was in any real interest in him I paid little attention to the way in which he was educated. I did not meet his teachers nor did I attend any parent evenings to find out how he was doing. I believe he was much influenced by his science master and the songs of Bob Dylan. He did not get the A-levels he wanted and ultimately dropped out of education and took off to the West of Scotland where he survived doing manual labour. He became fascinated by the teachings of an Indian guru and lived in a hut in Argyllshire, in a remote forest. Dorothy and I took our caravan to a nearby site and Timothy came to see us on his motorbike. He told us that we were no longer his parents and that he wished to have nothing more to do with us ever again. That was the last we saw of him. Sometime later he committed suicide and I think it likely that his rejection of us was his way of preparing us for what he was going to do.

The older son David did not do well at school and I suggested that he joined the Navy. He became a storekeeper and although full of ambition, always thinking that he could gain promotion, he was never able to fulfil his dream and after 22 years service left the Navy as a Petty Officer. We found him a flat in Chesterfield and he ultimately got a job as a forklift truck driver in a local factory. I did my utmost to build bridges back to him in an effort to overcome the damage I had done earlier by being too critical of his failure to achieve academic success. I'm sure now that he suffered from a variety of autism and that my criticism of him was entirely unjustified. He developed cancer of the liver and died in the local hospice and his long-standing girlfriend, whom he married just before he died, told me he had been an alcoholic; a fact he had managed to conceal from us very successfully. The poor man had suffered terribly because he had an older sister and a younger brother who were cleverer than him which did nothing to help his self-esteem. When he left the Navy and came to live in Chesterfield we got on very well and he was helpful and attentive, but the damage had been done.

To the extent that David was a loser, Erica, the oldest of my children, was a winner who benefitted very much from Dorothy's love and care. Dorothy was an expert seamstress and made clothes for all the children. She particularly enjoyed smocking and made some beautifully smocked dresses for Erica. Although in my own dysfunctional way I was not able to give her (Erica) the warm fatherly affection that was her birthright, I think Dorothy made up for it. After my experience with Honor I was determined that no child of mine would be unable to look after their children properly so insisted that before Erica struck out on her own, she undertook a nursery nurses training. Having finished that she decided she would like to become a midwife which she did, and later married Ron. It has given me much pleasure to watch how their marriage has progressed in Canada and I have been particularly thrilled by the family that she and Ron have created.

Yours fondly,

Pat

8

FRIENDSHIP

Dear Jack,

As a kid I spent a lot of my time alone. Being seven years younger than my brother and often left in his charge, as far as he was concerned, I was always a nuisance. At school I had only made one friend and remember being very envious when I heard people talking about their families because I didn't seem to have one. My father was not a family man and I suppose my mother was not either although she was the oldest of seven. At university I got on with people all right but again made no friends, so when I became a full-time psychologist it was no wonder that friendliness was something I thought about a great deal.

The insight that hit me hardest was the result of my asking myself whether I really liked the patients I looked after or only behaved as if I did. I don't know what made me ask that question but I did not like the answer which was that I was a sham. I behaved pleasantly because I wanted my patients to like me. I had what Berne called an 'approval hunger'. As a child I had not been given enough approval to make me feel that I was acceptable or likeable and was left with such a feeling of inferiority which could only be compensated for by me getting as much approval from other people as possible. This meant that if a patient irritated me (by not obeying my god-like instructions), I would cover my scowl with a pleasing smile and probably take it out on the kids when I got home. Seeing myself as I really was made it impossible to go on with this charade and overnight I stopped being nice. I had really been a sow's ear not a silk purse and if being honest meant that people did not like me, then so be it, there was no reason why they should. They could always go and see another doctor. In the event I did not lose any patients but my reputation changed. I stopped being that "nice" doctor and started being "that bugger will tell you straight". I had started by feeling thoroughly humiliated and ended feeling proud!

It took me a long time to realise that I was a loner and slower still to realise that the future of the human race depended on it learning how to be friendly. I had a sudden realisation of how unfriendly Homo Sapiens had become. It seemed that we only became friendly when experiencing some catastrophe like the Blitz in World War II, and when not facing such a threat to our survival we became unfriendly. It was at about that time it was discovered that our far off ancestor Australopithecus Africanus used bones as weapons with which to attack his brother. We have been fighting each other for a long time.

I realised that my difficulty with friendship arose from my deep feeling of inferiority. I thought that if people really got to know me they would not like me, so by keeping them at a distance and hiding behind a mask of 'niceness' I stayed safe.

When I started thinking about love and relationship I realised I was virginal. I was untouched! I had always thought that the Christian injunction to "go ye and love one another" was so out of reach of the ordinary person as to be not worth bothering about, and so easily passed over. But if for "love" I substituted "be friendly" then the instruction became not only understandable but achievable. I remember reading an account of the opening address to an American conference of student health by an eminent professor of psychiatry who said that if the world was to be saved "friendliness must be implemented soon". That was 50 years ago. I thoroughly agreed with him then and I thoroughly agree with him now.

Friendliness is part of our nature just as it is part of the nature of an elephant or a monkey or a dog. By nature we are friendly but our friendliness is easily repressed by the feelings of anger and hostility that arise within us when we are not loved enough as children. Some of Harry Harlow's unloved baby monkeys developed into the equivalent of criminal psychopaths. Some died, like many human babies in eastern European orphanages.

Human mothers vary in their ability to be affectionate and loving to their children. We could create a scale. At one end are those who are so damaged they are totally incapable of being affectionate, like Ben's mother. At the other end of the scale are those whose cup of mother loving brims over, and thank goodness for them. The general principle seems to be that the ability of a mother to love her children depends on the degree to which she herself was loved during the early years of her life.

One could say that where there is a lack of loving there is enmity and where there is love there is amity. I well remember being in the nether regions of a church in Sheffield with many other people during a bombing raid in 1941. We treated each other like long lost friends although we were total strangers. I was also very struck by the line in one of Shakespeare's sonnets "love is not love which alters when it alteration finds." This meant to me that there were two sorts of loving. One which depended on the other person living up to one's expectations and so could be called conditional; and another based on the lover finding the other a loveable person regardless of how he/she behaves and which is therefore unconditional. The fog was beginning to clear.

Surely the same could be said about friendship. It seemed to me that true friendship embraced the qualities of respect, tolerance, understanding and warmth, the characteristics of mother loving in fact. So far so good. However, friendship was not an attribute you could just turn on. But what gradually became clear to me was that the more I understood someone the more friendliness I experienced. To my great delight I discovered that I was becoming a more friendly person. This meant that I could stop bothering about trying to be friendly and work at deepening my understanding of people, which as a psychologist, I was doing anyway.

My final realisation was that love can grow out of friendship, as well as appearing at first sight like a bolt from the blue.

Yours fondly,

Pat

9

ABUSIVE RELATIONSHIPS

Dear Jack,

I retired from general practice when I was 61. By then I thought I had learned enough about emotional problems to start practising as a psychotherapist, which I did until I was 75. So I had two careers, GP and psychotherapist. I enjoyed being a psychotherapist more because I felt I really knew what I was doing, which was not always the case when I was a GP.

I became particularly interested in the recurring problem of abusive relationships. It was no wonder that I did so because after Honor's death I realised, to my horror, that I had been an abuser.

Whilst in general practice, a few women had come to see me complaining about being bullied by their husbands. I dealt with them as best I could, not realising that they represented the tip of an iceberg. It was not until my incarnation as a psychotherapist that I became aware of the size of the problem.

The women who came to see me at that time complained of feeling unhappy, inadequate and worthless. They thought they had a personal problem, not realising that they had been subjected to a sustained attack by their misogynistic husbands. The stories they told me had so many similarities that I can produce a composite picture.

She is a rather lonely lady with a low opinion of herself so that when she meets a man who is full of praise and flattery and gives her the full 'princess treatment'—red roses, candlelit suppers and all, she is overwhelmed. He goes on with his seductive techniques until she is convinced he is deeply in love with her and usually they retire to bed. They start living together in her mother's spare room (in those days) and all goes well. It is when they are living together in a house of their own that the trouble starts. His behaviour towards her changes. He becomes critical. He doesn't like her cooking. He doesn't like the way she dresses. She is sexually inadequate and so on, until she is completely demoralised. There are rows which continue until she breaks down in tears, and indeed which go on until she does which is the whole point of having the row. (Berne calls a row a game of "Uproar".) She thinks the way he treats her is justified because she is so useless, and it is usually at this point that she asks for help.

In order to understand what is going on here I'm going to produce a composite biography of the abuser who is a good example of someone in the grip of his Deprivation Psychology, in other words thoroughly mucked up.

He has a 'refrigerator' mother of which I could identify two types, one who is bad-tempered and domineering, the other a blackmailer. ("If you don't behave the way I want you to, you don't love me and so I will leave you", is the essence of the blackmail).

The son of the first type is argumentative and openly hostile, and that of the second is guilt-ridden, passive and compliant who will make every effort not to upset his mother. Neither sons have received any affection so they don't feel any and the closest they get to intimacy is in the area of sex. They both experience the dislike of the mother which is the inevitable emotional reaction of a child who reacts to his unloving mother as if she was dangerous and threatening to him, and this can become a dislike of women in general. A misogynist is born.

As an adult he has an affection hunger which he finds he can satisfy by behaving in a particular way. He is popular and the life and soul of the party, but deep down his dislikes lurk below his awareness. When he meets a vulnerable woman he wants to possess her and so switches into seductive mode. It is when she begins to behave in a motherly way, doing the housework, cleaning, washing, cooking that the deep resentments surface. He then projects the image of his mother onto his wife and tries to destroy her.

The mother of such a girl is not a 'refrigerator' but not terribly demonstrative either, and the same can be said for her father. The one intriguing finding in the abused woman's story was that she never experienced the affirmation of her womanhood by her father. She was never told that she was pretty or attractive and was therefore particularly vulnerable, and likely to fall for the man who offered her such compliments.

I always asked the lady to tell me about her partner's relationship with his mother. It was either very stormy, with many rows; or obsequious when he would pay more attention to the demands of his mother than of his wife. The blackmail was still working and he could only avoid overwhelming guilt by trying to please her.

On holiday the abusive behaviour stopped and he again became the charming person of the honeymoon period, no longer treating her as a mother substitute but as the person she really was. She was no longer doing motherly things. Thus the work of restoring the self-confidence of the unhappy lady who had come to see me started when I was able to show her that she had been the victim of the bad behaviour of a thoroughly mucked up person. The more I helped her to understand his life story, the better she became.

Then there was always a decision time, that is whether to stay or go and the direction of my consultation depended on the answer. If she stays she needed to be taught how to deal with the bully. To that end I would recommend books on assertiveness that would help her, and indeed I could teach her a few tricks like blunting the attack of the abuser by agreeing with the criticism. For instance, "Yes I am sure you are right. I am sorry to be so useless but I am doing my best and I cannot do any better!"

If the decision was that she wanted to go then we had to enter into a feasibility study the outcome of which was sometimes the realisation that she had to stay, but sometimes it was indeed possible to go.

There is one particular case that stands out in my memory. I knew the lady very well because she had come to me asking for help in a grief stricken state after she had nursed her much loved husband to his death from facial cancer. She was an intelligent and tough-minded lady and made a good recovery from her loss. She adapted herself to widowhood and took much pleasure in being a member of a local amateur dramatic society. When she came to see me again it was because she was in trouble with the second marriage. She had unfortunately married a seducer. The first part of their relationship was typical. He was full of charm and flattery and red roses and candlelit dinners. It is when they set up house together that his Jekyll and Hyde personality revealed itself. From being charming he could suddenly become critical and abusive and it was at that point that she came to see me. This gave me the opportunity to teach her how to cope with the bully without being upset. Being an actress she learnt to play this part to perfection. Her husband was also extremely jealous. He did not want her to have any friends or outside activities. He wanted to possess all of her. I knew that she could only survive if she kept up her contact with her friends and dramatics. His failure to curtail her activities made him very angry and the only time that he treated her properly was when they were on holiday. Ultimately he retired to bed and proceeded to drink himself to death.

The only way I could make sense of this was to suppose that the capture, the possession and the bullying was the only way he could avoid being overwhelmed by his own internal daemons, another consequence in the human male of being unloved as a baby, echoes again of Harry Harlow.

In extreme instances this scenario can lead to murder. For when the unloved child becomes an adult and finds a loving mate who gives him what his mother never gave him, he wants all of her and is powerfully motivated to want her to stay put. In his eyes his unloving mother was virtually absent and he does not want to be abandoned again. So his desire to possess her becomes overwhelming. If she objects or threatens to leave him the deep and buried hatred for his mother breaks out and he becomes murderous. The act of murder rarely occurs, but the potentiality is always there. A loving mate of the under-loved can neutralise such impulses, but I don't think they are ever completely extinguished.

Yours fondly,

Pat

10

THE ABYSS

Dear Jack,

I think this is probably the best bit of psychological work that I have done. At least it is the bit of work of which I am most proud! It has the effect of reinforcing my idea that the most important influence in our lives is the degree to which we are loved as babies. I think psychologists have skated round this one because of the fear that those not able to love enough would be criticised and branded as failures rather than being understood and helped. The fact remains that the degree to which we are able to love depends on the degree to which we, in our turn, were loved as babies.

Trying to imagine what it must be like to be a newly born baby is to move into territory where angels fear to tread but that will not stop me making the effort, something that the amateur can do but rarely the professional.

I had a friend who was the successful managing director of a local firm. When he retired, he retired to bed and refused to get up until the day he died. He told me that the thought of getting out terrified him and the only way he could find some peace of mind was to stay in bed.

And then there was Winston Churchill who said that he had attacks of the "black dog". Sounds very nasty.

And then there were the people who came to me because they were unhappy and who had been treated unsuccessfully for depression by GPs and psychiatry.

And then there was Ben.

Because I had time to listen, I asked my unhappy patients to tell me their stories and was surprised to find that they were not talking about the depression so familiar to me. They were describing sudden attacks of hopelessness, misery and the "no light at the end of the tunnel" feeling; despair, in fact, not depression. They talked about a feeling of being utterly alone, frightened and intensely unhappy and sometimes, but not always, angry. Extracting these stories was not easy. And I am afraid to say that the truth only emerged after much prompting.

These attacks would appear "for no reason at all" and would last for hours, days, weeks and then go as suddenly as they had came. When in its grip, the overwhelming desire was to go to bed and get buried under the bedclothes.

This was not depression. This was something quite different. Rather than attacks of depression, I called them attacks of despair.

Their family histories did not reveal evidence of neglect or abuse. Many said they had had a happy childhood but when I asked if they could remember any hugging and kissing, the answers were consistently negative. They had been told that they were loved but they did not feel that they were. I began to think about Harry Harlow and his un-mothered baby monkeys who grew up to be very disturbed. Some of them died. I began to understand the importance of 'bonding', the intimate relationship a loving mother makes with her newly born baby.

I found myself thinking about Ben and what it must have been like for him when he was born. I imagined him as a growing foetus, developing in an environment which was the best that evolution could offer. Warm, soft, elastic, full of a liquid in which he could float and move and kick, safe and secure. A feeling which would return when enfolded in his mother's arms, sucking at her breast, hearing her heart beat and the soothing noises that she made. Then I tried to imagine what goes on in the mind of the newly born child when he does not experience enfolding arms. I guess it is as if he knows that without them, he will die. Down the aeons of evolutionary time the newly born has been left out for the sabre-toothed tiger to eat. Left on the hillside to die, unwanted, and even today babies are still murdered. There is that within the child that remembers. So he knows he is facing the possibility of death. There would be trembling fear and utter aloneness. No response to cries for help, despair, defeat. Impossible to know about it for sure, but possible to guess.

When we saw Ben he was in a state of inanition with vital systems beginning to shut down. In his case there was no mother, no hugging, no cuddling to give him any sense of safety or security. But this happened when there was a mother, but one incapable of mother loving, who has been called 'the refrigerator mother'. As far as her child is concerned she is absent. Without mother love it is as if she is not there.

It was when I was working with despairing patients that the penny suddenly dropped. Could it be that their attacks were an eruption, a bursting into consciousness of the emotional component of the 'no mother' birth experience? When the newly born is anticipating the possibility of death? Like the fear of falling into a bottomless pit, an abyss.

My suffering patients had no idea why their attacks came so unexpectedly, but it did not take much searching to find that they were triggered by an experience of perceived rejection: an unfriendly look, a critical remark, enough (perhaps) to cause to resonate the emotional component of the original 'no mother' experience.

I think this emotional component gets buried below consciousness, banished to a place in the brain where it can do no harm, where it lies, not like a stone but full of energy like a spring wanting to uncoil whenever there is a chance. My guess is that it is buried in a part of the brain where it will not interfere with the functioning of the immune system.

I have often wondered whether Tolkien was re-telling an ancient myth when he had Gandalf the Grey fall off the bridge in the Mines of Moria into the abyss, and had to fight for his life with the fiery monster, the Balrog. His companions thought he had died, but, lo and behold he turns up later in the story as Gandalf the White, a purified and better wizard, (from 'The Lord of the Rings' by J.R.R. Tolkien.)

If the equivalent of the Balrog is a release of toxic energy, then the survivor can return free at last from the grip of his buried destructive daemon. I would like to think that this scenario is possible but at least I can say that in the cases I have worked with the severity of the attacks of the 'black dog' diminished when the cause could be understood.

A final thought about the malign energies that dwell in the depths of the mind. Sometimes the only evidence of their existence comes in nightmares. Blocked fear and anxiety can be expressed when dreaming about nightmarish situations. A looming catastrophe cannot be avoided but just in the nick of time there is rescue in the form of sudden wakefulness, heart pounding and sweating. The abscess has leaked, and dark energy released. Equilibrium restored. Somebody said that having nightmares prevents madness.

The person who is subject to such miserable attacks and despair is in bad need of the hugging and cuddling so disastrously absent from their lives as children.

Yours fondly,

Pat

11

GENDER PROBLEMS

Dear Jack,

Most of the people who came to see me were women. However, it was from them that I obtained much of my knowledge of male psychology gleaned from the stories that I was told by my lady patients. I did, of course, have male patients but it was only those suffering from depression who were completely open about their feelings. On the whole the absent males I was told about did not behave very well and apparently regarded psychologists as dangerous charlatans, in other words people who were not taken in by their charms. I used to ask the ladies if they would like to bring along their mates for a joint session but my offer usually fell on stony ground, the ladies not wanting anybody to know that they were visiting me. Emotionally upset women could ask for help much more easily than men who were much more uncomfortable about actually having emotions. As a last resort, there was always me to put on the psychological dissecting table!

I am certain that I am male and yet I am a hermaphrodite. I have nipples. And the same goes for women who have their vestigial penis. Both sexes were created by the coming together of maleness, the sperm and femaleness, the ovum. So I like to think that we have therefore two minds, the male active, outgoing, problem-solving and logical; the female, emotional, intuitive, receptive empathetic and creative. The influences of gender, physique and upbringing determine which mind is dominant. Looking at the four functions of the Jungian understanding of the mind, combining thinking and sensation belong to the male mind, and the combination of feeling and intuition to the female. Often male mind dominated patients would talk a lot and happily describe what had been happening in their world but would have great difficulty in telling me what they felt about these happenings. Apparently in some families emotions are not talked about and so the children have no words with which to describe how they felt. In which case I would produce a word list of emotions and was a witness to the extraordinary experience of people, for the first time, being able to put words to how they felt rather than just having to tell me that they felt upset. The recognition of and acceptance of the female mind had an extraordinary consequence for one of my patients, a very skilful and experienced sister in the coronary care unit of a teaching hospital. She began to have a bust, an outcome that delighted her but in no way was part of my therapeutic plan!

I found it much easier to introduce the male mind dominated people of either sex to their female mind but a lot more difficult to do the opposite. I would keep having to say: "Yes I hear what you feel but what do you think?" In the end the feelers would learn to ask themselves that question and so bring their male mind into play.

I suggest that there are three determinants which influence the characteristics of each mind; gender, physique, (I will write more about this when I talk about Sheldon in a few moments) and family influence. It seemed to me that the only one about which we can do anything is the last and that is where we would find the nature of our mucked-upness. It seemed to me that if our maleness operated in an un-mucked up way, we would be able to be active, involved in the affairs of other people, motivated by a desire to help people to be happier and not by a desire to dominate. It further seemed to me that the un-mucked up feminine mind would be able to motivate involvement with other people with a desire to encompass them, help them to feel safe but not to possess them. Having sorted that out made it easier for me to be objective about the way I behaved. I found plenty of things to work on! Assuming that we all want to bring up our children as un-mucked up as possible, our knowledge of their hermaphroditic nature would probably be helpful.

W.H. Sheldon wrote two books which influenced my thinking. 'The Varieties of Human Physique' and 'The Varieties of Human Temperament'. The work of this man has been discounted although the words he coined to describe our basic body shapes are still used: "ectomorph" for long and thin people, "mesomorph" for the muscular and broad, and "endomorph" for the rounded and plump. The great thing he did was to demonstrate that each bodily shape had its own temperament. For instance the ectomorph is seen as being sensitive and enjoying solitude; the muscular mesomorph, enjoying activity and adventure;—and the rounded endomorph, loquacious and sociable (and gossipy?)

The physique and temperament of the child is determined by its genetic make-up, which is why I think Sheldon is so important. It follows that the most damaging thing parents can do to their children is expect them to fulfil their (parental) unfulfilled ambitions when there is a genetic mismatch and the children are totally unsuited to such achievements. I know of a man who had a miserable childhood because his father wanted him to be a rugby forward when temperamentally he was suited to be a musician. He ended up by being a much mucked-up man.

Yours fondly,

Pat

12

PEAK EXPERIENCES

Dear Jack,

While I was in Sydney during the war a strange thing happened to me which I would like to tell you about. In order to understand it I must tell you a bit about my experiences with religion. My first wife, Honor, Erica's mother, was a theosophist, who considered that the great religions are branches of the same tree and embody the same underlying truth. Early in the 20th century they started a new Christian sect, called the Liberal Catholic Church (LCC). This had the same ceremonial and ritual as the Catholic Church, vestments, candles, bells and smells, but its operating principle was that anybody who wanted to worship would be welcome to do so, be he pagan, Jewish, Buddhist or Muslim. I found this very attractive. I had never been christened because my mother wanted to wait until I could choose for myself rather than being 'done' as an infant. I decided to join this church and was duly christened by one of its bishops (Bishop John Coates if I remember correctly). Later when I was waiting in a transit camp in Sydney for my next draft, I found there was an LCC Cathedral in Sydney and decided to get myself confirmed there. In order to prepare myself for this sacramental act I spent some time in the beautiful penthouse library of the Theosophical Society's headquarters in Sydney, reading and meditating. One day while I was there I began to feel extraordinarily happy in a way that I had never felt before and had the urge to go out for a walk. Once outside I felt I was at one with the world, with creation, an ecstatic feeling. I wanted to bless everybody that I met, including the sparrows! This ecstatic state of mind lasted until I had to go back to camp for a meal. It was only many years later when I read Abraham Maslow's book on religious experience, that I realised that what I had experienced was relatively commonplace and to which he had given the name 'Peak Experience'.

The experience had a lasting effect on me. It made me feel that in some way I was on the right lines, and that I was an okay person. I felt affirmed, an effect on me that has persisted. I have never had another such experience and count myself very lucky to have had this one.

Maslow talks about a 'plateau experience' with the state of the bliss of the Peak Experience lasting for days or weeks or for an entire lifetime. But it is not necessarily the result of experiencing Peak experiences but rather the result of prolonged spiritual discipline. As a result of his work he has found that there are those who have Peak Experiences and those who do not i.e. 'Peakers' and 'Non-Peakers' and he goes on to suggest that we Peakers are the prophets and the Non-Peakers the religious organisers!

It was such an interesting experience that I thought I ought to tell you about it. However, I don't think that one Peak experience qualifies me to be a prophet!

Maslow has written a book about it called 'Religions, Values and Peak Experiences', which he wrote in 1972 and which has been amended and reprinted many times and which I think is an extremely important piece of work.

Yours fondly,

Pat

13

GOODBYE

Dear Jack,

I have thoroughly enjoyed writing these letters to you. I know they have been very self-indulgent but in trying to introduce myself to you it could hardly have been otherwise.

I am no prophet and so I have no idea of the nature of the world you live in. What I have written is relevant to the world I live in and that alone might be of some interest. In any case may I say "bon voyage and goodbye"

I leave you with this poem by T. S. Eliot which I'm very fond of. Its title is "East Coker" and it is one of his Four Quartets:

So here I am . . .
Trying to use words, and every attempt
Is a wholly new start, and a different kind of failure
Because one has only learnt to get the better of words
For the thing one no longer has to say, or the way in which One is no longer disposed to say it. And so each venture
Is a new beginning, a raid on the inarticulate
With shabby equipment always deteriorating
In the general mess of imprecision of feeling,
Undisciplined squads of emotion.
And what there is to conquer
By strength and submission, has already been discovered
Once or twice, or several times, by men whom one cannot hope
To emulate—but there is no competition—
There is only the fight to recover what has been lost
And found and lost again and again: and now, under conditions that seem unpropitious.
But perhaps neither gain nor loss.
For us, there is only the trying. The rest is not our business.

I think that is beautifully put and describes my feelings exactly. My letters represent my way of trying to discover, once more, what has been lost.

My kindest regards to you

Pat

ACKNOWLEDGMENTS

It is with pleasure that I acknowledge and give thanks to all the people who shared the secrets of their lives with me and the friend's and relations with whom I have talked and sometimes worked.

In particular I must mention Tony Chesterman, Tony Winspear, Sophie Messer, Roger Moggs, and especially my late wife Dorothy.

I dedicate this to my first wife Honor, the mother of my three children, who taught me so much and for whom I did so little.